Personal Leadership Training Guide

Everything you need to know to think clearly, move forward and win with *Rules-Based Thinking*™

© 2018
All Rights Reserved

Daniel Gregory
PO Box 191
Medway, MA 02053
www.DanGregory.com

Yesterday's gone
Tomorrow's not here yet
What are you doing right now?

Contents

Preface	1
Introduction	2
1 – Please sir, IRAC some more	3
2 – The Rule for Communication	5
3 – The Rule for Team Building	11
4 – The Rule for Doing Things	12
5 – The Rule for Sales	16
6 – The 5 C's	17
7 – Wide and deep	18
8 – You win with people	21
Tell the truth	21
Trust, but verify	21
Manage on an individual basis	22
Attack the problem, not the person	22
Look forward, not back	22
Honor your commitments	22
9 – Become a Franchise Player	23
10 – Effective Living	24
Basic #1: Attitude	24
Basic #2: Activity	24
Basic #3: CCMP	26
Basic #4: Immediate action	27
Basic #5: Health	28
Basic #6: Relationships	28
Basic #7: Money	28
11 – Be, Do, Own	30

12 – True Control	32
13 – Nobody cares what you say	33
14 – You say it, you believe it	34
You become what you think about	34
15 – Leadership vs. Authority	35
16 – Price / Value relationships	36
17 – Master the basics	37
Everybody wants to be somebody	38
All you can do is all you can do, but all you can do is enough	38
18 – Keep a list	39
19 – Probability Events and Dynamic Risk	41
20 – Putting it all together	42
Stretch your mind	42
Expectations are the key	42
Leaders take 100% responsibility for communication	44
The winners have the same problems that the losers do	45
21 – You make it happen	46
Bonus chapter	48
Author's notes	49
Suggested reading list	50

Preface

As I see it, everybody basically wants the same things from life: good health, free time, extra money, family, friends and security. And yet when life is hard and we're struggling, it can sometimes feel like there's no way to ever achieve any kind of true or lasting success for the important goals which matter most to us.

But that's only one way of looking at things. Another way is to step back, start thinking clearly and start learning to win.

This training guide is a compilation of leadership ideas and tools which I've successfully tested for over 25 years. These tools have a proven track record of helping people do good things. Anyone who uses them can learn to think clearly, work more effectively and develop a stronger capacity to produce winning results.

My system of personal leadership is built on a methodology which I call *Rules-Based Thinking*™. Most of these ideas have a structure to them. And that's my plan with this book, to apply an organized structure to this collection of personal leadership training tools.

In my experience, the best way to teach new ideas to an adult is to focus on vernacular, reasoning and logical progression. And I think I've done that with this material. To the best of my ability, I've aimed my step-by-step presentation towards a single conclusion, which is this: *If you want to be a leader who wins, you've got to apply your attitude and activity towards delivering good results.*

Will this training guide be helpful to you? That's an open question and simply put, I don't know. I'd like to think that anyone can read these fifty pages and teach himself some new skills. And yet that's the curious thing about writing a book because no matter how valuable my ideas are to me; if they don't work for you too, by that measure I've missed my goal. But I'll let you be the judge of that.

Introduction

The system of this book uses a model which takes into account the value of both left-brain and right-brain thinking. With this method, you start with an outline as a framework of deliberate steps (*left*). Then you accept as valid only those thoughts and actions (*right*) which help you advance to the logical conclusion of your steps.

A Framework for Rational Problem Solving	
Left	Right
Identify problem	A problem is the difference between the current state and the preferred state.
Define objectives	Objectives are what you prefer, rather than what currently is, or isn't.
Generate solutions	Solutions are alternatives which can serve to give you the results you want.
Evaluate solutions	As you evaluate, compare the alternatives for speed, cost/benefit and feasibility.
Prepare best solution	Pick the option that's closest to your best price/value target; prep for that solution.
Implement	Most new process failures occur at the preparation or implementation phases. Be prepared to adjust in response to the unexpected; the goal is successful results.
Evaluate results	Check your work and re-loop from #1 as needed until satisfied with your results.

This *Framework for Rational Problem Solving* is a good basic example of a rules-based left/right logic constraint system. The steps on the left-side are an outline that functions as a logic flow to keep you on track, helping you stay focused. But the information on the right-side doesn't stand alone and it doesn't flow by itself; the right-side information is used to clarify the left-side steps.

Rules-based frameworks are helpful because they dovetail with the fact that people have a dual hemisphere left/right mind.

1 – Please Sir, IRAC some more

When you're seeking approval, results or help from someone who has official power, be it under the law or as part of an organization, there will almost always be some controlling rules in place. Because of that, it's often possible to frame a successful request along the lines of an IRAC argument, where IRAC stands for *issue, rule, argument* and *conclusion*. And since this book relies on logical framings, the *IRAC Framework* is a good place to start.

The IRAC Framework	
Left	Right
Issue	The *issue* is the situation being discussed. Optimally, it's your version of the story.
Rule	These are the *laws, rules* and *guidelines* which you contend should control the reasoning path towards a decision.
Argument	The *argument* is where you apply your facts and evidence in a logical reasoned manner to the rules which you cited.
Conclusion	The *conclusion* is where you sum up your argument and ask for specific resolution such as money, permission or help – or a sanction on the opposition.

A good argument can help you get results. But it's important to keep in mind that merely because you've got a winning argument, you don't have carte blanche to club other people into submission. Furthermore, there are two major shortcomings with the process of asserting a soundly reasoned argument:

1. Unresponsive people and unresponsive organizations do not have to pay any attention to you or your arguments. When you've got a disagreement which does not involve an enforceable contract or regulation, the other people involved can simply ignore you if they choose to.

2. Even if someone is obligated to hear you out and respond, it's a frequent occurrence that many people will be too busy, too inattentive, or too closed-minded to fully listen unless you explain yourself multiple times, remind them repeatedly or persuade them over time to agree.

But even so, I've found from experience that if you explain yourself with a soundly reasoned IRAC argument and if you give people time to think, they will tend to more easily agree. When you're both logical and persistently persuasive, other people will tend to cooperate – even if they think it's just to get rid of you.

Also, when you encounter a misinformed or closed-minded person who refuses to consider your request on the proper basis and/or who makes no effort to communicate honestly, there will sometimes be a means of appeal available. With an appeal, you can go over the head of the original person. But this takes time and making an appeal is always harder than winning up front.

Most organizations will tend to not fully address nuanced inquiries. Finely honed answers require candor and acumen. For this reason, you will usually be pushed away or avoided before you can speak with a decision maker, so keep that in mind and don't be impatient or lose your cool. If you express rudeness or anger at being roadblocked, you'll give the other party an excuse to refuse to help.

When I need help or I'm seeking specific results, I always reach out to the highest people possible. The higher in any organization you go, the better the chance you'll find someone who understands logical reasoning, and who, when presented with valid reasons, will accommodate you; especially so, if you find the right person. But if you do this at work, be careful to avoid stirring up trouble.

Bonus: Solving big problems will sometimes force you to seek help from others. When you need help, be sure to be specific but flexible in your requests – and don't burden people with nonsense.

2 – The Rule for Communication

The biggest factor in making things happen is expectations. Expectations are those ideas which fill in the gap between what is and what you anticipate will happen. But what does it mean to expect something? Expectations are forward-looking thoughts which are grounded in a likely to be true understanding of things.

If you studied a lot for your test and your professor is a fair grader, chances are you'll get a good grade. But if you don't study at all, on what basis is it reasonable for you to expect to do well? If the prep material is all new to you and you don't study it, then what?

If you don't exercise, should you expect to be strong? If you don't save your money, should you expect to have any? If you get drunk or stoned every day, should you expect to avoid having problems?

When you've got a hammer in your hand, everything looks like a nail. When you look for trouble, that's what you find. Expectations are a powerful force; so powerful they help make things happen, bad or *good*. And therefore, focused expectations have real value.

But how do expectations come to exist? In the search for the source of your expectations, you might look around or end up backtracking. And if you were to try that, you might come to see that expectations are caused by ideas. But what causes ideas?

The source of your ideas is twofold: those which you create yourself with your own thinking process and those which enter your mind from the outside by communication. But regardless of which source your ideas come from, all thinking, all information and all ideas (if you apprehend them) will cause expectations.

And this leads us to *The Rule for Communication*, which is what this chapter is about. Here's how it works:

The Rule for Communication	
Left	Right
Communicate	If you want to be a leader, it's your job to be sure your messages are understood via clear and effective communication.
Expect	It's not rational or sound to expect things from people unless they acknowledge you when you communicate with them.
Inspect	Based on what was communicated and is expected, one can inspect for compliance.
Reward	Most rewards are the verbal affirmations or criticisms which follow inspections.

It's probably not obvious when you first look at them, but the four steps on the left side of *The Rule for Communication* are a true algorithm which models all human communication.

Now I know that sounds like a mouthful, but unlike our first two left/right framings, the steps on the *left* of this rule are inviolate – they cannot be modified. In other words, these four steps are the way communication actually happens. But that's not to say you can't enter the cycle in the middle or otherwise cover the steps forwards or backwards. But it does mean all the steps are always applicable at all times and ultimately, none can be skipped.

Some people reject the absolutism of this rule and try to find ways to disprove it. But it can't be disproved because this is the way human communication actually works. And if this rule is true, then the wise choice is to admit that using it can improve your thinking skills, your communication skills and your leadership skills.

It's not possible to have expectations without first achieving an idea via communication. Expectations require ideas and ideas require communication. Ideas, even when they appear as a bolt from the blue, must connect in some manner with what we already know, or else we can't experience them.

Simply put, ideas cannot exist in a vacuum – they can only exist within the context of your understanding, and understanding is established by communication. Even if it's just you, thinking quietly to yourself, it's still communication.

From the perspective of leadership, the aim of communication is to establish a sound understanding of the issues at hand. Some issues will help you keep the status quo organized to your satisfaction. And some issues are actionable enough to help you move things forward. But in every situation, as a leader, it's your job to assure that your communication is clear and effective.

Here's a list of communication maxims (rules) which you should keep in mind (notice how these also have a left/right framing):

- **You become what you think about.** Communication is much more than just talking to other people. In fact, the most frequent personal communication in your life will always be you, thinking to yourself. When you're thinking, it's important to think carefully; avoid selling yourself short and avoid boxing yourself in. People do become what they think about – so keep that in mind. More on this later.

- **A soft answer turns away wrath.** This is actually a proverb from the Bible (*Proverbs 15:1*), but you don't have to be a religious genius to see the value in this. Basically, this precept (rule) says that gentle words and kind answers will tend to calm people down if they're upset.

- **You get more flies with honey than vinegar.** Every time I've found myself in a problem with people, especially bureaucrats, it's because we argued too much. Never get in a heated argument on the phone (or face-to-face), unless you have to. If a conversation goes bad, remember this rule and just hang up, or excuse yourself and walk away.

- **Don't kick people when they're down.** Over the years, I've made plenty of mistakes, but this is one blunder I've managed to avoid. From time to time, the bigger problems of life will sometimes get to people and when that happens, things can seem so bad that even a little problem is too much to bear. It's ok to boss people when you need to, but whatever you do, don't kick people when they're down. Nothing you're doing is important enough to justify beating up on the life, emotions or self-image of other people.

- **People worry about that for which they have no answer.** One of the more upsetting things people can experience is when they look ahead, but can't see how things will be ok for them. Fear of loss is the #1 motivator of people. And when the future is unclear, it creates fear of loss. As a leader, it's your job to allay reasonable fears by helping people to see a better way forward. But don't make a career out of catering to unfounded, irrational or greedy fears. Don't be a lame politician trying to buy votes by pandering to people with endless promises of wine and roses.

- **See one, do one, teach one.** This maxim is the best rule for helping other people to learn something. First, show them how to do it. Then, assign them a task so they can do it themselves. Lastly, put them in position teach it to another person. The best leaders are constantly on the alert for good opportunities to expose, involve and upgrade their team via the repeating method of *see one, do one, teach one*.

- **Always be willing to start again – carefully.** If you've been trying to communicate with someone and have been making no headway, it's ok to let things sit for a while and try again later. But don't arm-twist or beg other people.

Leave the gate to your friendship patio open, but remember that you can't force others to appreciate you or your ideas.

- **You say it, you believe it.** This rule is the most important principle of communication because everything you say affects everything you think and vice versa. From time to time, listen to yourself think. If you don't like what you're saying to yourself, then chances are you won't like the expectations those thoughts will tend to generate.

  Another key aspect of this rule is for when you give instructions. It's always important to make sure the other person repeats them back to you – to corroborate that the message was received. A verbatim read-back is the best acknowledgement. Less precise acknowledgements are also good, but the more precise, the better. A good rule of thumb is that you should never rely on anyone unless they acknowledge you and genuinely agree to cooperate.

- **Don't believe your own bullshit.** Exaggerating things so as to get the upper hand in a negotiation is a tried and true tactic. Everybody has done it at one time or another, and anyone who says they haven't is lying.

  But we also tend to exaggerate things as we negotiate with the circumstances of life. From a logical standpoint, these types of exaggerations tend to be ad hoc or post hoc. But both types serve the same purpose, which is to help us feel confident and correct in our self-affirmations about life.

  To avoid lying to yourself, it's important to review your thoughts from time to time. Everybody has a supply of what I call *lifestyle justifications*. These are the rationales and reasons we rely upon to justify why we live the way we do. Other than these justifications, there really is nothing preventing you from moving forward in life. So avoid empty excuses *and be careful to avoid lying to yourself.*

Probably the most important thing to keep in mind about communication is that there's real power in affirmations. We'll talk about this later in the book, but for now it's enough to know that internal thoughts work like the rudder on a boat. And that's why deliberate word choices are the right tool for deliberate thoughts and clear thinking. Choose your ideas carefully, but don't be shy about pushing forward when you're moving with urgency.

Many times, when you first meet with someone or talk with them their interface with you will be similar to that of a dried sponge. When you first pour water on a dried sponge, most of the water runs off. Likewise, when you first talk to someone new, most of your words won't sink in. This can be a problem when there are time constraints involved, so be prepared to repeat your message.

When it comes to effective communication, it's important to remember that your mind works best when it's clean, well-organized and smoothly running – like a good workshop. Don't waste your thinking on gripes, backbiting or angry complaints. And good communication takes real effort to establish, so it's especially important that you don't squander it with gossip.

Good leaders think clearly no matter what's happening. They never blindly rush forward in an unthinking panic. Even in a crisis, clear thinking beats panic; think slow or fast, but pay attention and *think*.

But thinking clearly is only half the battle. You also have to pay attention to detail and listen carefully. Good communication requires a sound basis upon which to communicate. And that means good communicators will excel at gathering information.

Bonus: If your ideas lead to stupid conclusions, change your ideas.

3 – The Rule for Team Building

The Rule for Team Building is great for moving people forward incrementally. The more times you apply this rule with your team, the better the results you'll get. If you use this in conjunction with *The Rule for Communication*, you've got a substantial amount of the basic tools you need to lead people and build winning teams.

The Rule for Team Building	
Left	Right
Expose	This can be formal, such as instructing someone to directly observe certain important details. Or it can be casual, where details are absorbed over time.
Involve	This is where you engage people in dialog, ask questions and have them participate either formally or informally.
Upgrade	An upgrade can be as simple as a kind word for a job well done (which would also be a positive reward) or it could be an increase in duties, pay, rank, etc.

If you get people involved in the process of developing ideas, they will be more likely to support the end result of that process. Involvement is the key to building support and it's the key to making appreciated progress with people. Don't just dump a situation in someone else's lap. Instead, with ongoing communication, involve them in the process of creating a solution.

One good method is to ask your team for feedback about your ideas and activities. This creates involvement with your team, and helps you spot problems in your plans and current situation.

Bonus: If you have to correct someone, use the *"sandwich"* method; start and end with praise, put the rebuke in the middle.

4 – The Rule for Doing Things

So far, we've seen a *Framework for Rational Problem Solving*, the *IRAC Framework*, the *Rule for Communication* and the *Rule for Team Building*. With each of those examples, we've seen that the outline goes on the left, and the clarifying details go on the right.

This style of left-side/right-side framework is why I chose the naming convention of *Rules-Based Thinking*™. But there's more to the story than that and since explaining it will help you get the most from this training guide, I'll explain it now:

In the introduction, I implied the possibility of there being a distinction between left-brain thinking and right-brain thinking. But to some researchers, that idea is unsubstantiated. At best, some say it's nothing more than conjecture or speculation. And because I'm not a brain scientist, I'm willing to concede that those experts may in fact be right. Thus, my ideas such as they relate to lateralization of brain function might not be empirically supported by widely accepted scientific proofs.

Even so, I'm going to plow right ahead and talk about left/right thinking because I'm satisfied to use non-scientific conjectures to support my argument. I'm trying to convey a concept which is sufficiently useful that it's irrelevant to me if it's provable by science or not. But as a point of clarification, think about this:

One of the books on my suggested reading list is called *Drawing on the Right Side of the Brain*. It's been about 30 years since I read the first edition of that book and I still have an old copy of it around my house somewhere. The author is Betty Edwards and she contends the right side of the brain is more adept at visually recognizing things. Extrapolating from that premise, her book teaches you to draw what you see, not what you think you see.

I know this method works, because from the little bit of drawing I've done, I've experienced it first-hand. And the results are truly remarkable. But for maximum effect, the impact of that book can't be merely explained, it has to be experienced.

Until you actually sit down with a pencil, quiet your mind, stop internally talking about what you think you see and instead draw what you actually do see, then you're not experiencing the lesson the author wants to teach you.

Somewhat conversely, I'm asserting that my method isn't so much on the right side of the brain, as it's on the left side. But similarly to how learning to draw on the right side is experienced by trying it, I want you to learn how to think on the left side by trying it.

When you undertake a right-brain drawing session, you draw what you see, not what you think you see. Conversely, to practice left-brain thinking, I want you to organize your thoughts around abstractions which are essentially algorithms for deliberate thinking – to help you know what you seek, not just what is now.

In this method, the right-brain is for fully and richly experiencing life as it presents itself to you. But the left-brain is best used for framing an understanding of how you want things to take place.

A color photo of your house is a right-brain idea. But the builder's blueprint when he built the house, that's a left-brain idea.

As I see it, the right-brain tends to take care of itself. It's always working and it's always ready to deliver a rich experience for us. All we have to do is pay attention and not talk over it too much.

But the left-brain, that's a different story altogether. And that's because the number one tool for effective left-brain thinking is an outline of carefully chosen words. And yet, because we use our words so loosely when we're casually talking and when we're randomly chewing idle thoughts, the proper balance of left/right thinking tends to fall into disarray.

With rules-based thinking, to make plans and move things forward you should draw up an agenda using left-side logical steps. But you should also be aware that there are already some pre-existing left-side frameworks which are so powerful and so perfectly vetted for correctness they should be accepted as invincible rules, because for all intents and purposes, they are. Here's a simple example:

The Rule for Doing Things	
Left	Right
Decide to do it	A decision to act must precede action.
Allocate the time	Doing things requires time allocation.
Do it	And of course, it won't get done unless you do it yourself, get help or delegate.

Look carefully at the left side. When doing things, is it possible to skip any of the three steps on the left? Because they are immutable, those three steps are actually a guiding structure, not a mere suggestion. And when dealing with rules, *you must use compatible logic*. But if you don't, then what's the point of having a rule?

With this system of left/right rules-based thinking, the objective is not to become an intransigent blockhead who refuses to yield when wrong. Rather, the aim is to transform some parts your thinking such that it's easier to stay on target as you implement activities which are aimed at moving things forward toward your goals.

By organizing your thinking into an outline and a clarification, you can more easily see that the outline is a summation of what you should be thinking about. And with that being true, if you're having trouble moving things forward, then you should ask yourself questions aimed at getting back on track, such as these: *What is my decision? What are my reasons? Why am I doing this?*

Most of the time, lack of progress can be traced back to indecision of purpose. If you're not working towards making progress on your agenda, then most likely you haven't made a clear enough decision to determine what your agenda is.

However, it's also possible to bite off more than you can chew. When that happens, even though you know what you want and even though you're working on a plan to get there, you can run into trouble if you can't manage your current workload.

On an individual basis, managing your workload consists of breaking down large problems into smaller ones, large objectives into a series of small tasks. No matter who you are or how talented you are, at any given moment you can only effectively do one thing at a time, so keep that in mind. Even a chess grandmaster playing fifty concurrent exhibition games at a big public event can only move one piece on one board at one time.

Even if you're working on multiple projects, working towards multiple goals, or even if you're simultaneously administering multiple programs, always keep in mind that at any given moment you must be willing to totally focus on the current task at hand.

Here's a good rule: *Don't expand beyond your management capabilities.* It's one thing to take on too much work and then have to cut back or get help. But it's another thing altogether to overwhelm your team with tasks they can't execute due to insufficient skill, or volumes they can't handle with low staffing.

The correct way to eat an elephant is one bite at a time. But there's no point in putting one on the BBQ spit if you don't have any firewood or kitchen help. Instead, start small now then do more later on. On the other hand, it's very easy to invent empty excuses to justify skipping hard work, so be careful to avoid that trap.

Bonus: Winners don't just quit. Instead, winners choose to win – they choose to keep trying; they improvise, adapt and overcome.

5 – The Rule for Sales

A sales process can be very overt, very subtle, or some mix of the two. Your objective might be to conduct a transaction, or you might only want to persuade someone to agree. Or you might be planting a message for a specific reason. Here's an effective rule for sales – but this is not the only one which exists or has value.

The Rule for Sales	
Left	Right
Attention	The first step in a sales scenario is to capture the attention of your prospect.
Interest	If people don't care about your message, they won't buy from you. A *no* can always turn into a *yes*, but absence of consideration always equals *no*.
Conviction	To precipitate conviction, you must plant your message deep enough to cause genuine thought.
Desire	If a person gets convinced about the merits of a proposition, they won't be able to put it out of their mind until they take action.
Close	When you close someone, what you are doing is locking in their interest and affirming their decision by agreeing with their reasoning process.

Searching for new potential clients is called prospecting. The complete *sales cycle* consists of *prospecting, approach, qualifying, appointments, presenting, overcoming objections, closing, delivery* and *referrals*. But always keep in mind that ultimately in sales, you get paid to prospect. Everything other than prospecting is academic and leads to failure, if you don't develop enough people to see.

Satisfaction is the ultimate test; if the customer's satisfied, that's great. But the best pathway to good customer results isn't only to make sure that all of your current customers are satisfied. Instead, the best pathway is also found by working hard to get more new customers. The more satisfied customers you have, the better.

6 – The 5 C's

Once you understand that getting people involved is the key to moving them forward, the next thing you need is an outline of benchmarks by which to measure your team. The idea is to focus exclusively on points which yield maximum results. When you use the 5 C's method, you get better results with people because you're looking for (and working to improve) the key aspects which matter the most in any management or team leadership situation.

The 5 C's	
Left	Right
Commitment	In any situation where real work is required, unless there's commitment, things never get started. Or if they do, they eventually go astray and/or fizzle out.
Coachability	When you lead people, coachability is essential. It's always better to work with people who are coachable and with people who are willing to cooperate.
Capability	Ultimately, you must develop capability to cross over from failure to success.
Caring	If you want to lead people or build a team, you must care about the mission, the people and the results.
Continuity	At all times, your team's well-being and your focus on the mission must be protected from disruption.

Ultimately, it's *capability* which tips the scales. But at any given moment, *coachability* is the most essential attribute for a team builder to focus on. A person lacking talent, if they're coachable and if they're committed enough to keep trying, can still do well.

But a person with a bad attitude, who won't cooperate – that person is bad for your team and should be avoided, even if they are very talented. Team builders don't build on uncoachable talent.

Bonus: An effective way to test for coachability is to assign your team some unpleasant tasks and then observe how they react to it.

7 – Wide and deep

Whenever people and things are involved in a system, the true relationships between the elements can be understood by using a wide/deep visual chart. Here's an example:

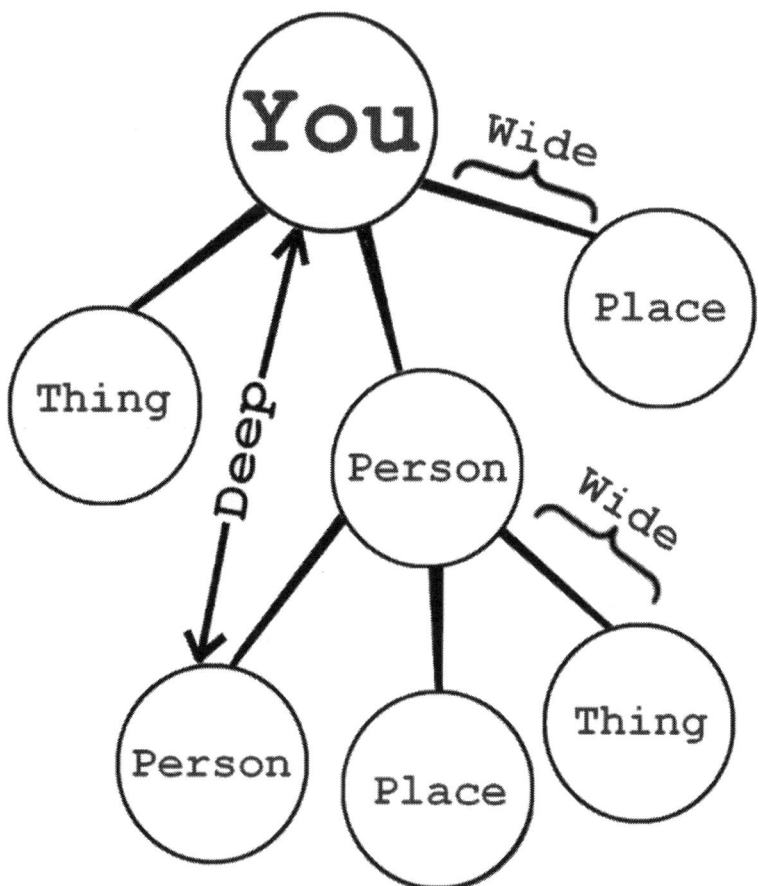

Anything directly connected to you is *"wide"*. Everything else is *"deep"*. These are not mutually exclusive, but the dominant relationship controls. Most of the bigger problems in life can be solved by expanding your circle of top quality direct connections.

Bonus: There are only two directions in life: *wide* and *deep*.

The only relationships where you can exert any direct influence are those which are wide (direct) to you. In every other situation, in order to put your wishes into effect or advance any influence over a situation, you have to go through at least one intermediary.

The deeper the level of the person you try to rely on, the greater the chance your instructions will be diluted or your preferred course of action won't be followed. The closer you are to the action, the better your position when you want to exert leadership.

As a leader, your job is to move the mission forward. And the best way to do that is to keep your boots on the ground where the action is. If you stay on a friendly first-name basis with your key people and if you communicate with them regularly, it's a lot easier to influence their actions when you need to make things happen.

Another interesting thing about the wide/deep modeling system is the mathematics aspect. In its simplest form, the math of the wide/deep framework can be understood this way:

At any given moment, each wide connection (*person/place/thing*) in your life has a price/value net which you can estimate. And at any given moment, the value of that connection can be expressed as "x". And when you're investing yourself into a relationship, your aim is to increase the value of it from 1x to 2x, etc.

But there's also an alternative: Instead of trying to drive a wide connection from a 1x to a 2x or a 3x value, you can simply add more connections and reach your objective that way. If for example, you require 20x of total value to have a sufficient support network such that you can pursue your objectives, as an alternative to increasing the value of your current connections you can simply add-in the value of some additional connections.

The greater the number of worthwhile wide connections you have, the less risky your life will be and the more opportunities that life will present to you. Provided that you proceed carefully, good things will almost always result from going wide.

When it comes to connecting with other people, "wide" is where the action is. The connection links between people will always be the source of your best leadership results (and biggest challenges).

If you look back at Chapter 2, you'll see that *The Rule for Communication* does have a definite structure to it. And I can assure you that I've accurately presented this structure. In other words, *communication* does lead to *expectations*, etc. But even though the structure of the rule is clear, the ramifications are not – not unless you think about them in advance.

Whenever you're dealing with other people and before you start talking to them, always take into account how you're feeling, how busy you are and what your message is. Then factor in an expectation that the other person is also facing a set of potential communication challenges. And on top of that, remember that most people have no experience with structured communication, so they might get upset if you try to hold them to account for the logical conclusions of a discussion (or worse, for a reprimand).

Effective leaders make consistent efforts to take into account that ad hoc communication links are not reliable until confirmed. Unreliable links should always be approached very gently.

Only when you have a reliable link with someone should you ever try to persuade them forcefully or impose on them substantially. All other people should be handled with kid gloves at all times.

Reliable wide connections are best established with friendly attitudes, true commitment, clear communication and honest effort. And please keep in mind that reliable wide connections are hard to establish and are therefore, very valuable. Don't squander them with stupid ideas, unfair impositions or excessive complaining.

8 – You win with people

When dealing with people, the best rules to follow will focus on honest dealings and doing right by others in a deliberate manner.

Tell the truth

Don't withhold important information, don't equivocate and don't dissemble. Be intellectually honest, be forthright and don't hide behind your authority when you're wrong. Don't be ad hominem; don't make people or personalities the issue. Focus on the truth of the subject at hand. When faced with truth, receive it gladly.

But don't be a blabbermouth. A good rule to follow is this: *Never give people so much additional information that they have trouble processing it.* And if you're trying to persuade someone, then as soon as it's clear they agree with you, stop talking or change the subject. Don't derail a closed sale; don't talk yourself out of a sale.

Trust, but verify

Good personal relations do require friendly behavior, but they do not require that you blindly accept everything you're told. Sometimes, people will have incomplete information and other times, they'll have wrong information. Not only that, but people will often shade the truth – especially to avoid being embarrassed. And sometimes, people will flat out lie to you.

In your new life as a leader, you'll often have to make a choice from competing alternatives. But choosing wisely requires that you verify the information you are basing decisions on.

It's a fool's errand to try to run on a broken foot and likewise, you should not try to rely on false or unverifiable information.

Bonus: Use the 5 W's; *who, what, where, when, why* (and how).

Manage on an individual basis

As a leader, you will have objectives which will require you to pursue activity and get involved with other people. And there is no escaping this fact: *pursuing personal activity in our modern world will put you into contact with other people.* But people do differ in basic style, in self-image, in emotional stamina and in capability. Therefore, you should manage your interactions with others on an individual basis. This means that methods or solutions which work right for one person might not be the best fit for the next person.

Attack the problem, not the person

When dealing with ordinary people – people who are just trying to get through the day, be deliberately careful to cut them slack whenever possible. Attack the problem directly. Don't focus on the other person's faults. Instead, focus on resolving the problem.

Look forward, not back

When dealing with people problems, discuss the problem, agree on a resolution and move forward. But don't hold on to any grudges. Don't endlessly dredge up past issues. Don't endlessly carry around a mental grievance list for future gripe sessions. If it's bad enough to be a problem, then it's bad enough to deal with; but deal with it directly, and then move on.

Honor your commitments

If you follow this principle wholeheartedly in everything you do, it's almost impossible to fail long-term in any situation.

By sharing your strength with others through reliability, you lessen the burden on others and make things better for everyone.

You can be the worst bum in the world, but the very moment you start honoring your commitments, your life will start changing for the better. Smile, keep helping and don't quit; resilience is the key.

9 – Become a Franchise Player

If you want to become the leader of your life, your #1 objective should be to invest yourself in the ongoing task of increasing the viability and durability of your personal franchise. And by franchise, I don't mean a fast food business or your right to vote. Instead, in this context, what I'm referring to is the sum total of all the thinking, learning, ability, effort, stamina, skills, resources and relationships which you can draw on and utilize towards the task of keeping your daily life in good order and functioning well.

In my way of doing things, it's more important to have durable personal franchise than it is to chase after a consumerist life of merchandise-driven fake satisfaction. The idea here is that it's better to start small, with something that works. Keep your life organized and functioning well, and build from there – carefully.

You can think of your personal franchise as a secret clubhouse where you can rest up, study, and learn to be a winner. The daily grind is challenging and learning to be a winner is hard work. But when you have the resource of a strong foundation, life gets easier.

The best skills to develop are those which will help you live effectively now and improve your life over time. Here's a list:

1. Attitude
2. Activity
3. CCMP
4. Immediate action
5. Health
6. Relationships
7. Money

These are the key basics you should master, if you want be strong instead of weak. We'll look at them in the next chapter.

10 – Effective Living

Many good opportunities and lucky breaks will come from unexpected sources, so it's a good idea to be on the lookout for them. And yet, lucky breaks won't make you a better person. But training yourself with *The 7 Basics for Effective Living*™ will.

Let's look at them in detail:

Basic #1: Attitude

The single most valuable asset you can have is a winning attitude. *A winning attitude is a results-driven mindset that feeds on positive expectations.* The best way to stay motivated at your job is to have a plan for positive winning progress in your personal life, and to work on that plan every day. The best way to cooperate with others is to avoid aggressive behavior, stay out of ego battles and smile.

- You don't have to go to every fight you're invited to.
- Life will give you whatever you are willing to accept.
- It's easier to wear slippers than to carpet the whole world.

Basic #2: Activity

The best way to organize your time and effort towards optimal results each day is to divide your thinking into four types of time:

- Activity
- Resting
- Chores
- Goof-off

The key idea behind results-oriented time utilization is that you have an objective in mind, and only those tasks which effectively contribute to achieving your objective are counted as *Activity*.

For example, let's say you're putting sandbags in place on the riverbank to help keep the levee from overflowing. In a scenario like that, your personal efforts (your *activity*) would consist of:

- Obtaining sand
- Obtaining bags
- Filling them
- Putting them in place

As long as the flood crisis was pending, you would do nothing but work until you drop, filling and stacking sand bags – these actions count as *activity*. But if you eat or sleep, it's only a brief amount, and that counts as *resting*. If you sweep up a small amount of sand for a sense of cleanliness, that's a *chore*. If you stand around smoking cigarettes and daydreaming, that's *goofing-off*.

The idea behind focusing on genuine activity is to help you live by an optimized price/value system. Superior results are obtained when we focus our best efforts on making good things happen. Each minute that passes without real *activity* is a lost opportunity.

There's very little value in goofing-off, so people should do very little of it. Resting is ok, but goofing-off is a real waste of time and money. Likewise, chores are also ok; but once we see the difference between *activity* and *chores*, then we begin to understand the importance of living a life free of useless things.

Everything you own and everything you do requires input and upkeep from you. Whenever you are engaged in chores-oriented busywork, you have that much less time & effort available to focus on doing better activities with real potential for winning progress.

Almost everything you own is a net financial loss. Only income producing assets and appreciating assets have the potential for net gain. And even among those, most will take lots of time & effort for upkeep. Similarly, almost everything we do is nothing more than busywork. Very little of what people do in a typical day is real activity aimed at producing agenda-advancing results.

I recommend that you do only those activities which are aimed at helping you move things forward, and less of everything else.

If you work hard, live right, save your money and if you assign genuine winning activity to be the top priority of your life and daily efforts, everything else will eventually start to fall into place.

Bonus: The *80/20 Rule* says that 80% of your good results will come from 20% of your activity and 80% of your problems will come from 20% of your situations (and people). So be on the alert for this rule; do everything you can to work with it, not against it.

Basic #3: CCMP

CCMP is an acronym for *Clear Concise Mental Picture* and it's the best way to stay focused enough to accomplish something worthwhile. When you concentrate on keeping a clear, concise, picture of good results in your mind, that mental picture helps you see what you want and it helps you stay motivated to win.

But even if you're living an honest life and you're being good, if you make yourself too obvious (or if you get too pushy), most people in authority will treat you like an adversary.

For most people in power, a small person trying to step up and do better in life is seen as a bad thing. For this reason, it pays to avoid attracting attention, and it pays to keep your mouth shut.

If you're not careful about whom you share your dreams with, you might accidentally spill your guts to unfriendly people who don't support your aspirations and are not interested in helping you do well. Worse yet, you might share your dreams with someone who is actively seeking to keep you down. And if you do that, you're giving them a road map so they can rain on your parade.

Whatever your objectives are, you have to think about them very specifically, and very concisely. Develop a clear vision in your mind of what you want, and focus on that every day. But be discreet – do not go around bragging about your plans for life.

Basic #4: Immediate action

An immediate action list is a quick list that you make right now, with the aim of finding something productive to do right now.

Here's how it works: Let's say at some point during the day, you find yourself sitting around, not making effective use of your time. Grab a notepad or sheet of paper and write down the three most important things that you know should be done right now.

Then look again, and draw a line through two things that will take the most time or will be the hardest. This leaves you with one thing. As soon as you see what that one thing is, get up and start working on it immediately. If time allows, repeat the process.

Don't fart around, don't get distracted and don't overthink. An immediate action list is not a goal-setting session. Rather, it should take less than three minutes and the objective is to help you see the next most important thing you should be doing right now.

Basic #5: Health

Of everything in this book, good health should be the most obvious. If you get sick and die, life is over. Take good care of your health: Don't smoke, don't drink, don't take drugs, don't sleep around, don't overeat and don't drive recklessly. Wear your seatbelt, avoid trouble and avoid crime. Eat healthy, do more exercise, stay fit. Learn, adopt and live by this creed: *mens sana in corpore sano*. Think good thoughts, reach out to help others, save your money. Floss your teeth. Don't get tattoos, don't ride motorcycles, don't do dangerous things and most importantly: *Don't live like a fool – don't force your life into bad situations.*

Basic #6: Relationships

Your goal in life regarding other people is to interact with enough of them such that, from the stream of people you meet, there will be at least a few who are a good enough fit for you to develop winning relationships with. When the chips are down, it's good to have friends. And a good way to keep your pool of interpersonal relationships fresh and invigorated is to keep an eye out for new faces and new friends. Building good friendships pays dividends.

Basic #7: Money

Because I did investment and insurance planning for almost 25 years, I've got a pretty good handle on this one. And based on that experience, here's a list I think you should follow:

1. Stay out of debt
2. Stay out of debt
3. Stay out of debt
4. Earn more, spend less
5. Appreciate what you have (literally)

6. Multiple sources of income are a good thing
7. Speculation is very risky, don't do it
8. Sell some of your unneeded possessions
9. If you work for a living, don't buy luxuries
10. Don't take equity out of your home
11. Don't borrow from your 401k
12. Don't splurge on junk
13. Invest in people – good people are better than money

For leaders, money is something to be saved, not spent. The secret about money is that it's repelled by those who complain about not having any. But it flows to you when you focus on being prepared, doing the right thing, working hard and hanging around with clear-thinking people. Making money is like getting infected with a fungus; once it's on you, it tends to stay there.

When it comes to money, if you keep trying long enough, you'll eventually accumulate some. When that happens, keep on saving and investing. Don't rush to spend. It's a lot harder to make money than it is to spend it – so keep that in mind.

The three best investments are: own a business, mutual fund IRAs and carefully helping deserving people in a prudent manner. But if you are going to invest in individual stocks, your best bet is to learn a good deal about *free cash flow, dividends, debt service, trend following* and *buying on a pullback.*

Back in the 1970's, everyone was freaking out about inflation and the oil embargo. Now, people are freaking out about job losses and health insurance. Ten years from now, it will be something else. Your best bet is to ignore all that, work hard and save your money. To make money, find something that works and do as much of it as possible. And remember: it's better to make 50 cents than nothing.

Tomorrow will be here soon enough and it's a lot easier to face the day with a cash nest egg saved up, than when you're broke.

11 – Be, Do, Own

In order to introduce the concept of "Be, Do, Own", I'll first explain the kids' game known as *Rock, Paper, Scissors*.

What you see in the illustration are three hands, each forming a representation of different things. The closed fist is *rock*, the open hand is *paper* and the pointing fingers are *scissors*.

The rules are simple: with stack-fisted countdown of "*1, 2, 3, shoot*", each player makes a hand-shape, and then they compare:

- Rock crushes scissors
- Scissors cut paper
- Paper covers rock

There's never any mistake regarding who wins in a game of rock, paper, scissors. Similarly, with the *Be, Do, Own* system, there also is no confusion – not unless you want to be confused.

You can think of your life as being a small rowboat with two oars. The boat itself represents "*Be*". One of the oars represents "*Do*". And the other oar represents "*Own*".

- If you try to *Do* too much, you'll go in circles.
- If you try to *Own* too much, you'll go in circles.
- If you don't live right, if your *Be* is messed up, your boat will leak, leaving you in panic mode to avoid sinking.

At each point in life, the verifiable state of your *be* is what you are. Likewise, if you want to *do* something, you have to do it or else it's not you doing it. And you either *own* something, or you don't.

I know it's a hard thing to accept, but there really are only three ways to experience life. And that means, for all personal growth and goals, the only variables you can invoke are *Be, Do* and *Own*.

Contrary to popular belief, it is possible to be happy even if you're poor. But if doing lots of fun things and owning lots of nice things isn't what makes people happy, why is everybody always chasing after expensive toys and good times? Is that all there is to life?

To me, the right amount of money to have is enough so you can have a nice nest egg, help your family and help your friends. More than that is still good, but money alone is not the solution to life.

Likewise, the right amount of socializing and fun to have is enough so that you don't go crazy with boredom or end up living alone as a hermit because you refuse to spend time with other people.

And this leads us to the curious conclusion that the best things to do and the best things to own are those things which help you better manage the process making the best of life, every day.

Ultimately, if you want to be your best you should live right, do the right thing, and own a game plan for making personal progress.

12 – True Control

One of the most misunderstood words in life is *control*. People tend to think it only means to boss others or to have authority, but it doesn't. Here's a simple fishing diagram to explain it:

When people are in a boat and they're slowly motoring forward with a fishing line being pulled through the water behind them, that's called *"trolling"*. And based on this diagram, we can see that *control* can be thought of as meaning *"to resist being pulled"*. Therefore, *con-troll* is a useful mnemonic device.

Think about the larger forces of life: *laws, rules, bosses, other people, etc.* Each day, real world external constraints limit our choices. Thus, the impact of outside forces must be dealt with.

As a leader, sometimes your best available choice will be to *"get along by going along"*. But other times, especially when you're working on your own personal plans, the best option will be to exert a *con-troll* solution against the interference of outside forces.

Bonus: Instead of fighting with reluctant people who refuse to get with the program, replace them with someone else who's willing to cooperate. And don't try to impose control on impossible situations. Instead, focus on doing everything you can to make things right – then leave everything else to take care of itself.

13 – Nobody cares what you say

If you can't communicate your message well enough that others will accept it, the net effect will be worse than nothing. You will be seen as an annoyance and will be intentionally ignored.

This can sometimes be overcome by persistence, but if the other person is unprepared, too busy, or too dishonest, he will move to stop you from trying. These attempts to block you will sometimes be an invocation of formal authority, but more often it will be a brush-off like *"stop bugging me"* or the excuse that there's not enough time now (is there ever?) to discuss things to a conclusion

But incomplete communication leaves people with unanswered questions. And as long as questions remain unanswered, people will tend to worry or be anxious. It's as if they are trying to think a full sentence, but an important word is missing.

What if you were to think *"I know my children are safe tonight because they're staying at _____'s house"* – what effect would that missing word have on your mind? People truly do worry about that for which they have no answer. And therefore, when you are talking with people, your aim is to put their mind (and yours) at ease with leadership-oriented dialog.

When you are leading people in a dialog, your job is to steer the conversation to topics and ideas which will help them see the solution for themselves – without you explaining it too much. Ask questions which make people think before they answer. Ask questions which help people see the answers for themselves. Assign tasks which help the other person discover on their own how to best move things forwards. Don't just tell people the answer. Instead, help them see it (*and think it*) for themselves.

Nobody cares what you say– people care about what they think.

14 – You say it, you believe it

This principle works through the power of affirmations. But the problem with affirmations is that most people invest too much thinking into bad affirmations and not enough into good ones.

The idea behind self-directed affirmations is that you've decided you're sick & tired of listening to the old boring soundtrack of complaints in your head, so you choose better thoughts instead. Deliberate self-affirmations produce results because the power of good thoughts is inherent. Good thoughts = good expectations.

You become what you think about

This rule teaches you to say good things to yourself every day. When you say it, you think it. If you think it, it becomes true.

- "I look good, I feel good, I am good"
- "Right now is the best time to get started"
- "The more I try, the better I get"

Here's a good acronym to think about: *TIGER*™. I suggest that you spend some time every day talking to yourself about this. Take a moment right now, and repeat this phrase in your mind:

"Today, I get excellent results."

T oday
I
G et
E xcellent
R esults

15 – Leadership vs. Authority

Having authority is like owning a pit bull that's been rescued from the fighting pits. You own the dog, but unless you're good with animals there's not much you can do to reform it or help it learn to be gentle. But leadership can be equated with being able to carefully rehabilitate that same dog, bringing out the best in it.

When you have a role which is recognized as having an official capacity giving you "say" over other people, then you have authority. But when you use your ability to produce worthwhile results, then you're a leader. Anyone can just trudge along through life, bossing others and/or being bossed. But only leaders can assess situations, add focus and shape results for the better.

Generally speaking, the majority of people who have authority are not leading anywhere near their potential. This shortfall creates opportunity for new leaders to emerge in almost any situation. However, weak leaders will tend to actively oppose a newcomer who has equal or less authority, so always keep this in mind. When trying to lead with initiative, watch out for entrenched naysayers.

Whenever there's conflict, use this rule to help avoid mistakes:

1. Don't be a jerk
2. Keep the mission in mind
3. Use power gently as a tool for compliance
4. Respect the limits of your authority

Bonus: People tend towards three basic styles of understanding life and relating to each other: *thinking, feeling and sensing*. But many of us are often not aware of how this affects us or how we express ourselves. Therefore, good leaders, good managers and good friends will be tolerant – and give people leeway. It's much easier to lead your team when you're helping them find the way forward.

16 – Price / Value relationships

Unless you have no alternative, never invest your time, effort or money into any situation where you don't reasonably expect there's a good likelihood of producing worthwhile results. Don't spend your entire life investing everything you have into bad price/value relationships. In a good relationship, everyone involved makes an ongoing best effort to deliver win/win results.

Periodically, for every relationship and every situation in your life, you should ask yourself this question: *"What price am I paying, and what value am I getting in return?"* But please understand that I am not telling you to measure the cost of your relationships and throw them overboard if they fail your price/value test. Instead, what I'm saying is that every circumstance, every aspect of every situation, and every relationship, can be measured in price/value terms – and those values must be taken into account.

Any price you might try to pay is limited by the total amount of personal "oomph" you have available. *Insight, initiative, stamina, diligence, compassion, money*, etc. – these are not inexhaustible resources. You can stretch yourself again and again, but at any given moment, all you can do is all you can do. It's not possible to do more than you can. But the implicit tag-along to this fact is the realization that the right amount to do is all that you can do. Never settle for half-ass results. When doing things, always do your best.

Good leaders work towards objectives via a process of admitting the truth, setting sound expectations, holding people to account and assigning honest price/value measurements. But good leaders will always give team members multiple opportunities to improve themselves. And this means that even when you're pushing people for better performance, you must *never, ever* dump someone before coaching him and giving him multiple chances to improve.

17 – Master the basics

Back in the mid 1980's, I was a rep. associated with the A. L. Williams Regional Training Center in Framingham MA. At the time, I was still young but was very lucky that the Regional Vice President for that office was a company leader and an excellent sales trainer. Under his leadership, I learned enough to be competitive and was frequently a top producer in the office.

The thing I enjoyed the most about that training was the Wednesday morning managers meeting. Those meetings went from 9 AM until 12 noon. Each week, the RVP would drill common sense and sales methods into our young skulls of mush. The meat of what we learned was a series of *basics*. These basics were a portfolio of precepts, maxims, napkin presentations and various rules intended to help us do well.

Because basics can be so effective, we spent a lot of time in training class learning them and doing drill-for-skill, week after week. To us, knowing the basics was so important that we even had a basic to help us remember to use the basics: *"Master the Basics, never get off them; make changes slowly, if and when"*.

I think this precept is self-explanatory, but if not, here's how to understand it: Once you've mastered something that works for you, stick with it; do not recalibrate without serious deliberation.

Basics can be as simple as a precept which tells an important truth, or as complicated as a napkin presentation. The diagrams in Chapter 7 and 12 are good examples of napkin presentations. Here are a few precept-style basics, from a variety of sources:

"Nobody owes you anything"
"You can't get something for nothing"
"There's no such thing as a free lunch"

"People support that which they help to create"
"The speed of the leader is the speed of the pack"
"Life will give you whatever you're willing to accept"
"You make it big by letting others make it little"
"It's easier to get forgiveness than permission"
"People like people who agree with them"
"People eventually seek their own level"
"Why do you say that?"
"If I... will you...?

Some people actually go through life with an ethic of *"Me first, screw everybody else"*. But don't you do that! Stay on the alert – don't ever let a selfish attitude take root in you or on your team.

Everybody wants to be somebody

This basic is sufficiently important that I'm singling it out for additional explanation. This rule states that everybody, even people who look and act like losers, wants to be somebody. As a leader, your job is to look at everyone as if they have a neon sign on their chest which says "treat me right, appreciate me".

For a lot of people, it's not very often that they get any praise or appreciation – so don't be a phony with too many compliments. But do make the effort to say something nice from time to time.

All you can do is all you can do, but all you can do is enough

This particular basic is the title of a book by Arthur Lynch Williams, Jr. If you read his material, you will see that several of my precepts come directly from him. I'll leave it to you to figure out which ones, but what I will tell you is that some precepts (such as this) are not mere conjectures; they are facts. But this particular basic is the most powerful in this book. It's an attitude statement of true winning power: *You can't do any more than all you can do. All you can do is all you can do, but all you can do is enough.*

18 – Keep a list

To give yourself direction now and over time, it's important that you keep four running lists. The lists start with the most transient, most current, and they end with the least transient. Here they are:

1. **Urgent.** These are the brush fires. These are the things which must be done today so as to avoid problems here and now. Put gas in the tank. Pay the electric bill. Feed the dog, meet with an important customer, do a task for the boss, etc.

2. **Priority.** Generally speaking, these are things which you know you should do right away but haven't gotten to yet. This is a dangerous place for things to land because more things fall through the cracks here than anywhere else. Another name for a priority list is a "to-do" or "backlog" list. For the most part, things end up on your to-do list or in your backlog pile for only three basic reasons:

    a. It's today's workload
    b. It's left over from yesterday
    c. Spill-over from your urgent lists and plans lists

    Try to avoid spinning your wheels on leftover items of limited value. It's better to go tackle a new elephant than to spend a whole day sweeping up old mouse droppings.

3. **Plans.** Plans are not goals and they are not mere chores. Neither are they wishes, shopping lists or guesses.

    The best use for plans is to solve problems and make progress. A plan starts with a written expression of the results we seek to obtain. Along with this expression, we make a list of every known step we might take and every resource we possess, which we might put into service to achieve our objectives.

Then the list is organized around what's most feasible and re-organized into logical, bite-sized steps. Each step is double-checked for feasibility and refined to eliminate any useless deviations and/or to take a better approach. Once all of that is in order, the purpose of a written plan is that it acts as a punch list for the discrete steps needed to produce the results we seek.

4. **Goals.** Goals are the *raison d'etre* of the leadership mind. A well written list of goals is better than a suitcase full of cash. If there's one single fact you can learn from history, from other people and from life itself, it's that people tend to veer off course over time. If you want to be a leader, then staying on target is where the rubber hits the road. And to stay on target, you must set goals – and you must work towards those goals.

Executing a best-efforts work list follows this model:

1. Get serious
2. Make a list
3. Get started now
4. Work until you drop
5. Repeat

And keep in mind that when you write down a backlog cleanup list or an *immediate action* list, there are three categories to think about. Those three are *"fast", "slow"* and *"too much for right now"*.

But no matter what you do to vet your thinking or set agendas, it's important to write things down. And that's because the process of making a good list is, by itself, a significant contributor to making progress, moving forward and winning. A written punch list serves as your personal left-brain agenda of activities. By making a list and working on those items, you avoid the distraction and wasted time which inevitably follows when there is no plan of action.

Bonus: Good ideas + paper list = incremental action good results.

19 – Probability Events and Dynamic Risk

According to generally accepted probability theory, a *sample space* is the set of all possible outcomes to an experiment. And an *event* is a subset of the sample space under examination.

Think about looking for the last granola bar in your kitchen cabinets. In the most simplified sense, the sample space is all the cabinets in the kitchen and the event is the cabinets you look in. The total number of possibilities in your life is your personal sample space and the size of that space is much larger than you think it is. For every opportunity that you know of, there are at least several others which are just as good, maybe better.

Every single moment of your life is (and can be) a discrete *probability event*. Every single day, every single hour and every single minute gives you multiple chances to apply yourself to the best of your ability – and thereby drive outcomes in your favor. Every instant of time is an opportunity to take winning action. Leaders don't just "give in" to bad luck. Instead, they apply themselves to the task of changing things. When you change your circumstances, you change the possibilities of your sample space.

Most good decisions made about bad surprises are helped by the clear thinking which comes from specific training. But most bad decisions are made when people react without local information.

To avoid making bad mistakes when reacting to risk or danger, use the OODA loop: it stands for *Observe, Orient, Decide, Act.*

Observe what's happening, orient your thinking to the immediate facts (and your training), make a decision and act on it (keep re-looping very quickly until you're sure the real trouble is over). But very few surprises constitute real risk or danger. Therefore, in most situations the best initial reaction is to remain poised; take time to think carefully about your best choices and your best outcomes.

20 – Putting it all together

Let's assume for a minute you've read this book carefully and you're convinced that accomplishing things in your personal life based on goals, plans and a deliberate activity punch list is a good idea. Even so, there still remains the question of where to start – what should you focus on first? If I was forced to choose and I could only keep a few of the ideas in this book, I'd keep these:

- Clear Concise Mental Picture
- Rule for Communication
- Winning Attitude
- Lots of Activity

I'd pick these because these four basics are so essential that if you were to only focus on them, you could still be an effective winning leader. But since it also helps to master a wide variety of skills, in this chapter we'll recap some things and fill some gaps we missed. Your first goal should be to convince yourself winning is possible.

Stretch your mind

Your mind is not like a rubber band; once you stretch it, it does not return to its original position. As you learn and grow, your inner fears that you might slip back into excessive self-doubt will go away. Once your mind has been stretched, it does not go back to where it was. The old you goes away and the new you starts today.

Expectations are the key

When people think and form ideas, part of that process is the forming of expectations. Armed with even a snippet of information, the human mind can draw upon its inner database and weave a visually rich, logically sound conception which rolls out in front of us like a red carpet. Before you experience the future, it doesn't exist for you. And before the future exists for you, you expect it into existence. That's the recursive aspect of the forward thinking human mind – it really is true that you make it happen.

Here's an important secret for you: *whatever your mind can conceive and believe, you can achieve.* Your life, regardless of how far it might be from how you want it to be, can be converted and improved through the forward-thinking process of having the right expectations. But good expectations start with good thoughts.

Good thoughts yield good expectations and good communication has two forms: *self-talk*, whereby we talk to ourselves, and *interpersonal communication*, whereby we interact with others.

When we talk to ourselves, what's happening is that we're using our own words to shape our own expectations. And when our expectations are met, we congratulate ourselves. Conversely, if we fail to achieve that which we were hoping for (expecting), we tend to criticize ourselves. But when we interact with others, a more precise and deliberate use of that same principle becomes clear:

- *Communication* should, but does not always, precipitate reasonable expectations.
- *Expectations* should, but do not always, prompt logical inspections.
- *Inspections*, even if they reveal unmet expectations, are the process whereby we verify what transpired; trust but verify.
- The ending step of a communication loop with another person should always aim to be a pleasant closing acknowledgement. This acknowledgment is a *reward* for the other person's effort invested in conversing with you.

Bonus: If you need to calm an upset person, use the 3 R's; *Repeat, Reassure, Resume.* Never try to *resume* before you *reassure.* But please understand that cajoling and demanding are not substitutes for listening; stay alert for the warning signs of emotional fatigue.

Pleasant communication and overt praise are both forms of positive rewards. Conversely, negative rewards can include unpleasant conversation and chastisement. Though it's not always essential that you immediately criticize poor results, it's always a good idea to promptly praise a job well done. Excessive criticism is called *managing by negative reward* and should be avoided.

Leaders take 100% responsibility for communication

As a general practice, leaders do not guess unless they have to. Instead, leaders keep the conversation focused on clarifying information and agreements, so they can develop accurate expectations. Leaders avoid the habit of stumbling around in a misinformed state. However, not all expectations and plans are a good idea. Please think carefully about this proverb:

"It is pleasant to see plans develop. That is why fools refuse to give them up even when they are wrong."

Proverbs 13:19 (Living Bible)

The prime objective of effective leadership communication with yourself and others is to insert your team into a process aimed at making successful progress towards good results. And remember this: *when you're working alone, your team is you.*

Rather than doing all kinds of foolish thinking, I recommend that you adopt a single premise and think deeply about that one thing. Then block out everything else and focus on only that preeminent thought, taking action as needed to bring that thought to a logical and productive conclusion. Think about winning good results.

As a leader, it's your job to make sure that your message is understood. Don't let people just "yes" you to death – inspect their understanding by querying them. And listen carefully to the answers; over time with enough dialog, things will become clear.

The winners have the same problems that the losers do

The difference between winners and losers is that losers think they are the only ones who have problems. Losers refuse to accept that people who persevere also have problems. Losers cling to the false premise that their problems are so uniquely debilitating that they are doomed to defeat forever – and so they never truly try to win.

But when you finally begin to accept that everyone faces problems, and you start understanding that your problems are no worse than anyone else's, then thoughts like *"it's too late"*, *"it will never work"*, *"I can't"* and *"I'm afraid"* will get reduced in rank.

As you continue to learn, work and grow, even though you'll still experience occasional doubts, fear will no longer rule the roost. Instead, you'll experience new thoughts and better ideas. And those new winning ideas will be simple, but powerful:

- *Every day is a new day*
- *Every time I try, I get closer to success*
- *Inch by inch, it's a cinch*

Winners don't let setbacks defeat them. Instead of accepting defeat, leaders follow the steps of *The 5 R's*™.

1. Review (your results)
2. Reaffirm (your mission)
3. Regroup (your plan)
4. Reapply (yourself)
5. Resume (good activity)

The best way to get ahead of problems is make multiple attempts as needed. In this context, an "attempt" is a unit of effort, a single iteration. Don't just try once, try 10-20-30 times or more. If you land in the ditch, stop; clean up, regroup yourself and start again.

21 – You make it happen

Although most of my early career experience was in sales and small business, the kind of leadership I'm talking about isn't only related to the sales/business arena. But there is a very strong connection in my methods to one particular area of the selling process, so it's important for me to explain that connection.

The selling which I've done a lot of over the years involves applying systematic effort to locate new customers. And over most of my small business career I consistently obtained a good number of satisfied customers as a result of that type of deliberate effort. I've done the prospecting, made the presentations, closed the sales and delivered on my promises. From soup to nuts, it's been those steps which have produced successful results for the customers.

But of the steps involved in selling new accounts, there's one key linchpin and without that, nothing ever happens. What I'm talking about is the efficacy of the sales presentation.

In true direct sales, the entire selling process rises and falls on the client presentation. When you're face-to-face with potential customers, it's your job to influence their thinking sufficiently that you can effectively plant your message. In other words, you must disturb their current sense of satisfaction enough that they will genuinely consider the alternatives which you are presenting.

Of course, people are free to accept or reject your message – and they are also free to accept or reject you. But while you are there, while you are talking to someone, your job is to intently press your message into that person's thinking. And the more effective you become at planting your specific message, the better your results will ultimately be. But if you fail to plant your message well enough that it takes root, you have not done your job.

My system of personal leadership rises and falls on that same idea: *the effective communication of a specific message.*

If you want to lead people, it's not enough that you merely convey a message. Rather, you must effectively communicate your message. And by communicate, I mean to actually transfer – the same way one microorganism can transfer DNA to another.

As a leader, effective communication is your true job. Therefore, when you talk with people, unless you're just relaxing with friends there's no room for idle chit-chat. Each and every time you're talking with someone, your job is to know what your message is and you should look for ways to plant that message. And even among friends, leaders look for edifying ways to lead.

For example, I never let a day go by without finding a way to point my wife's thinking in the right direction – and validate her as a worthwhile person. Why? Because my job as a husband is to make life better for her, to keep making things better for us, and to keep the both of us moving forward together as a team.

Similarly, when you have a team of people you're leading – even if they don't know you are leading them, your job is to point them in the right direction. Your job is to reduce problems, pat people on the back, move things forward, and produce good results. In other words, it's up to you to make good things happen.

I've got a slogan button pinned to my office corkboard which says "Nothing happens till someone sells something" and that's a true message. Likewise, in business, in your personal life and at home, nothing ever happens until you produce good results.

The process of leading yourself and other people to improved results always starts with a clear message and that message is this:

Know what you want, allocate the time and get started now.

Bonus chapter – Winning at work

The Rule for Being a Good Employee:

1. Show up on time
2. Keep a smile on your face
3. Do your work with sincere effort
4. Cooperate to the best of your ability
5. Improve yourself over time

PAPER – *People, Ability, Preparation, Effort, Results*
TEAM – *Together, Everyone Achieves More*
SOAP – *Subjective, Objective, Assessment, Plan*
HALT – *Hungry, Angry, Lonely, Tired*
SBI – *Situation, Behavior, Impact* *
(**Caution: Total commitment is digital, but empathy connections are analog*).

The Empathy Voice Safety Valve: *"You seem upset... What can I do to make this situation go better for you?"*

Diversity Rule: The difference between difference is equal.
(Difference ≠ Deficient; Difference = Difference).

The Tiger's Paw					
Person	*Power*	*Approach*	*Attach*	*Win*	*With*
Head	Own	Thinking	Contribute	Planning	Learning
Heart	Be	Feeling	Connect	Teaming	Loving
Belly	Do	Sensing	Participate	Responding	Leading

1. Good leaders plan ahead
2. Good leaders have an agenda
3. Good leaders seek win/win results
4. Good leaders count excellent results as the best outcome

Empathy Leadership ABC's:
　　　Appreciation *(show it)* **B**efore *(seeking)* **C**ompliance.

Author's Notes:

I probably should have found a better way to fit these final few points into this book, but I didn't, so here they are now:

1. No lying, no cheating, no stealing.
2. People are happy when they think they have what they think they want; winning is the art of living well with this.
3. Be kind to your web-footed friends, avoid antagonizing people. Daily life is not combat, don't trample people.

The easiest way to avoid having problems is to avoid having goals or dreams – and to content yourself with whatever life gives you. But if that seems stupid to you, then the only alternative is to take life one day at a time, working hard and making improvements on a daily basis. I recommend that you adopt this four point plan:

1. Build on core competencies and good relationships
2. Read, think, set goals; look forward to good things
3. Stay focused and sharpen your winning edge
4. Apply yourself daily anew

Your winning edge gets sharpened when your winning attitude is diligently applied to solving the problems of daily life. Applying yourself daily anew means to admit your faults, commit to improve on them and to work on your goals every day. And lastly, since we started with left/right structured frameworks, let's finish with one:

A Framework for Winning Each Day	
Left	Right
Go to bed early	Don't stay up late unless you're working
Be prepared	Keep your house, clothes and tools ready
Be serious	Be deliberate, stay focused, do your job
Be humble	You are not perfect, please allow for this fact
Think about tomorrow	Each night, take time to reflect; appreciate your life, commit to improve, commit to win

Suggested reading list

The Gypsies – Jan Yoors

Boone – T. Boone Pickens

Kabloona – Gontran De Poncins

Rhinoceros Success – Scott Alexander

Looking Out for #1 – Robert J. Ringer

Shantung Compound – Langdon Gilkey

To be a Good Printer – Gaylord Donnelley

You Can Negotiate Anything – Herb Cohen

The Templeton Plan – John Marks Templeton

How to Sell Anything to Anybody – Joe Girard

De Bono's Thinking Course – Edward De Bono

Origins of the Bill of Rights – Leonard W. Levy

The One Straw Revolution – Masanobu Fukuoka

Drawing on the Right Side of the Brain – Betty Edwards

The Man Who Mistook His Wife for a Hat – Oliver Sacks

Euell Gibbons' Beachcomber's Handbook – Euell Gibbons

A New England Town: The First Hundred Years: Dedham, Massachusetts, 1636-1736 – Kenneth A. Lockridge

Audio: Rogers' Rules for Success – Henry Rogers

Audio: Goals – Zig Ziglar

Made in the USA
San Bernardino, CA
27 May 2018